NOT NOW NOW

RESCUE PRESS

CHICAGO | CLEVELAND | IOWA CITY

NOT NOW NOW

Copyright © 2025 Sandra Doller
All rights reserved

Printed in the United States of America
FIRST EDITION
ISBN 979-8-9886839-2-6

Design by Sevy Perez
GT America & Graveur Variable
rescuepress.co

Sandra Doller

NOT NOW NOW

for Alphie
most loved

NOT

I had to stop stop
I was stoned I was stoned out out
I didn’t
I didn’t zoom oom
I was in an other way
an other place
before me

Down the line
down the sayable line

Who toughed
the tufted brush
Hard who had that landscape
membered

Their alma critics
suffered a sayable thing

We happy helpless gathered
our jars a door
our mouths
tiny rottens

+

Had to click the blue blue
Hop on pop ops
I had a killy mcfinger
too oo
I had a girl

on a yard on a car

Rooster beasty taste me
Tumble to the forgettable

That's the red spot
right there stop spot
The red spot I mean
the red stop—
in the bush

Who ain't got no blue left no
crumble

Who ain't you took to
yet

Her pass-
port pho-
to, this ch-
anges every-
thing

+

I know you too
too well ell
to leave you a-
lone with a figure
finger
Blue signage in the breakage

someone stop age
ageing today

A brown cluster is you
husked happy
inside big hilarious
I'm starting to see things
I'm not sure I'm seeing
I know that one
is coming at me

Let's stay inside the game
shall we
You take that brown
I'll take this
We'll call it
"Personality"

+

Pray for me mister
for I have thinned

things down a bit
on the sides

Attack of the figural painters
Attack of the hidden containers
Attack of the muscadine cokeheads
Attack of the forty-five signage
Attack of the canted perspective

Attack of the dashing blue beasties
Attack of the door without closure

Attack of the men
of the two-fisted too fast men

Woman—wummin—I
told you to get yr blue ess
down here and sign my check
and kiss my cheek
and signal my beginning
and tell me what to wear
and give me a wedgie
and stifle my guitars
and stipple my sassafrass
and wheel my loungecar
and wipe my crested elblow
and abscondify my monies
and salute me how to salute
and watch me do this
and that

You were a sign
in the distance
going fastest

+

Hard day for shorts.
Yump.
It's leaning time.

Hand pocket hand pocket
pock pock hang.

Peek a blue dailyness about
it, the gets.

Mudded crusty butte
Springs.

Too much land much land
in here.

Had to be
interrupted.
Usted.

+

Back away
from the smokestack
old people
might get turned

Does no one say
good bye
no more
Where is that man
a come for

+

Hot cross the mouth a prosey situation sold it to the wilds tilly till the white spotted lines on the faces add up to yours and your situation. Alice here the first time comes, she the second comer. Talk to me over the round numbers. Take a beating. And I mean home with you.

+

Walk this way, 30 clicks. I can see me from afar now, momma. I'm eating dice again, real big. I've got the gape tooth eye sucker in my face, poppa, what is your table made of? Who told you you could get this close?

+

Back away back away let's see your back away. Too much rhythm on the highway equals meat. Too much meat meeting street. Too much of you, too much a me. Too mean to give it up, take it back, climb the tree and spy the hole halo whole around your body. Ground.

+

Who said come to play like that. Play like that. Tan like that. Who said walk the line like that. A blue blue corner on the earth. A split slit goer walking backwards. We are going in reverse. Don't stop us yet, we are almost not not there yet.

+

Mrs. Aptitude: We don't want no incidents. We want a medium amount of incident.

Beauregard Yella: It's about the way we get along. Get along. Long.

Mrs. Clean: Jonathan, take that tooth out of your mouth this instant. Wash that gravel with your face.

+

One more series
of nowhere anyone is climbing
for free

Just give me
one more series

I'll carry
the weighted
broken things

+

Have you ever heard the one about the spaceship and the goat?
The racket and the lexicon?
The gangster and the grass?
The pocky and the aeroplane?
The cutout and the string?
The wrestler and the twig?

The plunger and the fist?
The straight shot and the broken glass?
The network and the organ?
The tie dye and the rollercoaster?
The distance and the tree?

+

That's a lot
of puddles.

Can't have too
many.

It's just that it
sits there.

So wicked.
Slick.

+

There goes the A-list
into the forest

Here comes all
Niagara

We're all falling into
a painting

We're all smashed smashy up
against it

+

It's good good good
goody good

Here here here here
here

So long seminal
building blocks
DNA smoothee

It's been a line line
line time

How could it not
have folded

The difference between the news
reporters and the internal

documentarians is one of
timeliness.

Let's say I want this
out there now.

Now.
Like already.

Let's say I wish I'd already
said it.

Had it eaten, consumed, drunk
for breakfast.

Let's say good and done
and onto the next.

Out with the
rest.

A paragraph is not a problem
a poem is.

It's not like I sit around
yesterday's news.

But years gone by, remember
paper yellows.

Please deliver me the 1930s
New York Times by noon.

Do you read the news and think
you can have some impact on the news.

Are we talking affect or
effect.

Do you read the news
whatfor.

We watched for four
years until we stopped.

We kept waiting for it to
stop don't stop.

We are trapped like tele-
grams from another time.

We hear people talking
out the window and

go to close it.
We do.

We are trying to record.
Fortunely.

I have spoken to my colleague in this way
and received no reply.

I am worried there will be
mandated togetherness.

I heard you had a party
and it was inside.

It is possible the entire house
is being eaten.

Forces seen and
un.

I need to be un if I am to be
at all.

I am talking career ending
in a way no one

from the future
will understand.

Maybe I mean
the past.

Maybe the future will be all
about career ending.

Before you take a step
take a leap.

Dummy didn't make the thing
you think he did.

He lifted up his arms
and we all felt it.

We all felt good
for him.

To leave behind his scandal
of trees.

He levitated and orbited around
the driveway for a while.

Until his career
really took off.

Without commentary
or favor.

He was a success
of his own kind.

Never wrong,
always night.

Gilded a little
among the palms.

+

The longest day poem
is Irish in its lone o

a loney tame temperature
afraid of its own ladder

We live in heat
A place of no season
How many of you have no
salt to spare

I saw three non-birds a morning
My chickadee cried in her kindergarten classroom in our
house a home

We have no visitors no inviting hours
no more
We have chairs and chairs and want
more

When she is sick I write
What kind of mother
is that

No kind

+

Yes we have
no perspective we
know we have no no

White people
didn't see it

coming

That's a lie
we saw it
the ship
defines
the shore

White people
oui
are sad
to find out
about it

My students
think I am
too specific
about it

They don't
know the literature
about mother
hood

There is no
literature
about mother
hood

+

Crown found.
Your child is not
your problem.
Be still my
Swedish heart.

Mama don't
worry is a tautology.
We have a birth
right to blight.

I want to get out
of the country but
I also want a pool.

I have to look up
how to make your
dog flip flops.

The child will like
the way other people
are. I'm better than
some, not as good
as others; I'm very
good at all things
I most hate to do.

This is your condition
not my problem,
the form states.
I pay the bill
with relish, the cost
a small coin,

a baby's tooth,
another visit
another day.

I can't tell my child
the names of those
trees, not only be-
cause I don't know
but because I've lived
this long and not want-
ed to.

Why are stories about
boarding school so
exciting? Insert notes
on nature here.
There's something
so wrong with a
prolific poet.
Especially a girl.

You and your dirty
I. Remember the belt-
less napkin you dug
out from someone's
grandma's undersink?

What is it I can do
it, says the man not
doing it. I am not like
other mothers—real.
The day she says she
hates me is near.

I found a crown
and another and another,
four drowned crowns
down, I tested them
for symptoms of regal
disease.

All negative all
done all
clear.

On the one hand
you have to wake
up every morning
as if you're going
to wake up every
morning again; on
the other hand you
have to act like this
is your last breath
in case someone
is taken away in
the night or on the
street. When you see
someone driving in a
movie you know they're
going to die. I tell my
child she will live a
hundred years as long
as she doesn't text and
drive or drink too much
or drugs or get too sad
or drown or dive into a
shallow pool or forget
to look both ways but
even then there's no
guarantee. How long
can I keep her from
knowing this. My father
is still alive but so many
are not alive, count the
ones who died before
him and should not
have, who did not de-

serve to die while he
does he does deserve it.
Everyone knows
children do best
when their parents
hate each other.
We need a common
enemy.

+

They say
the queen is dead
I say
long live my father

I use face cream
I use heavy cream

Conservative is to save
progressive is to mooch
tendu is to stretch
they say
I don't say

The law doesn't take
into account the actual
puzzle of being
A Woman

The law says I say this

The law says I am two
chromosomes in
two fingers deep
I say I am one double
X problem X marks the
slot

My father has not accounted for
the queen
The empire is wearing
a fancy hat and bright
colors so she can be
seen

The mother is too busy
to tell you why

I can't see outside
the frame of my own
substruction

If I'm funny or wear a
funny hat maybe you
will hear me over the
water I put in your
ears when I pushed
you out of me

My father thinks he
made me, I say
the queen did

They say it's always difficult

for the party
in power
to hold on

Have they met the queen
my father
"The child was the father
of the woman"

You always wanted
to do your best
for her
they say
But she was only a female
boss
She was only an
empirical example
of what's wrong
and of what
is

It's the custom
that steers
the ship you don't even get a say
And that's the way
fatherhood functions
the queen
the father
the nation

That systems work
beyond us
is beyond me

is the promotion
perpetuation of
paternal order
That parentage
travels on the
why
how ridiculous
to loosen
the tie

The queen is always
your father's mother
there is some honor
in just persisting
to exist

Everyone needs a queen
everyone needs a wife
every man should strive
to be both

What does it mean
to never complain
if feminism
is a complaint against child rape
forced birth
makeup and bras
domestic labors
outside
employment
demanded or denied
double time double
jobs double boobs

hand and blow and suckle
one and the same
never complain
to me about your
never complaining

I keep thinking
there will be
a female takeover but realize now
from here on in
it's only kings.

I wish that I knew what I know
Rod Stewart knows now, I wish
I had his everything, especially
when he dolls it up for me, a flick
of a bang to the sky. How did Rod
Stewart get the way he got and how
does he not stop being that way.
Rod Stewart is a stand in for our
mother issues and our lack of
understanding of corporate
taxation rates, historically
speaking. Rod Stewart is everyone's
worst vision for their child, like
who cares about the genetic
test that will tell me if I've got
a thriver or not, what if I have
a Rod Stewart inside of me, growing
now as I speak, knowing what he
knows now that he didn't know
then that we know he knows now
when he wasn't even beginning
to know it. Sometimes at the base
of my skull I can feel Rod Stewart's
comb plucking a tangle, teasing
a feather from my hairs. Rod
Stewart on a tire swing, Rod
Stewart inside a tunnel, Rod
Stewart watching TV, Rod
Stewart driving on the wrong
side of the street in another country.
Rod Stewart is not me and I am not
him yet, but I am still growing and I
do not yet know what I knew then

when I was watching the news a lot
in bed. There is no way Rod Stewart
has a normal sized bed just like there
is no way some very large men have
regular sized toilets. There are just
some things you know and then there
are just some things you don't.

+

Flaming in the installation
museum the one with the
mattresses on the walls and
the big pink puffy bed and
pillows and the art of dark-
nesses and they say minim-
alism can't be beat unless
you try. The number of
Russian artists trying not
to make a statement out
numbers the number of
everyone else. Three steps
forward into the polka
dot turns you into a cat.
These are the muumuus
you wear for yourself
and these are the ones
you wear for someone
else and this is how you
put on your glasses the
wrong way so everyone

knows you know what
you're saying. The ones
deep inside the café wear
the best overalls patted
over all with abstract tulips
sakura daffodils buttercups
and other common spring
wearing flowers. Political
statements you can truly
sink your nose into, like
an installation on the very
top floor you walked miles
to get here together and
the guards watch you watch-
ing their phones. You could
really get into this if you didn't
have to be somewhere else
soon. Everyone is talking
around you about how they
don't know what they're
doing. The tiny white socks
someone took time to sew
individually covered in beads
they look like little penis
covers or maybe hoods
tiny ones. You want to
take a picture of these
ladies in their large match-
ing print wear that could be
from Finland but isn't. It's
from here. The sick sock
sculptures represent the
Catholic church and their

abuses. Ties to ropes from
the ceiling dangle them
at your knees and shoulders
at first sight looking like a
bunch of bowed head flow-
erring classic rock cloths,
at last reading themselves
into the century light, blue
light, red corners, white mid-
dles. The note at the end of
the line explains everything.

+

I'm a likeminded liker of likes
stave yourself
from the Pams

If you had a Skeltonic
you'd sell it for a
brick

When women speak with
their mouths full of soap
call a barber
your daughter

Their mouths wide
whale for the credit
card insert a flag here
here no here

Wommins are staging
themselves from each other

You can't break a thing
like that they say you can't
stop on A or THE you can't say
UM or ellipses or exclamation
forbid once in your life please
stop using them and sign in as
Guest only I could go on and in
I could go for it in prose but I

But I but I don't like saying I
so much I like a thing more
central less centric more puffed
lilac and bushy toed it all makes
adds if you make it

Let the times you flinch be
the times you're really in it

Once I called a steak a steak
and let it stand in

There are some very short
with tucked in tube tops and
very long hair and huaraches
that look like a very different
season you think you could thin
it out and she seems elegant
like an 8th grader like someone
you remember from when you were
then

You were never then
You wore a kilt and safety pins
down the side as if you were a Ramone
himself

Black and white opera really does it
Takes you back to the top

Remember the time you taught
your child how to roll
over and over on the orange bed
her orange hair bleeding into it
from inside her vintage suit
bought by a woman named Sue
Sue Bee the tallest coolest
motorcyclist kind of woman
with the short stacked hair
like this line stacked to make
a thickness a thinking thing
is not a writer is a barista is
a theme here some kind of
thyme you lacked in your
recipe and didn't pack your
cups

Keeping you in them
cups
Not going past them
gates
You're already hemmed
in
No need to flaunt
it

We don't talk about
you know

She could revise all the
way
back to the office to get
a refill
but she'll just leave that
there

On the way home you notice
he doesn't use the word I
at all, just We and They
occasionally You but never
Himself never inserted as if
that's a kind of absence
when in fact it's the worst
kind of present tense
takeover as if he is not even
in his own likeness

She puts on a sunglass and prevents
herself from this century
In this way is she formed
over and over like a shell

She thought it was one song
but it's another now and the mood
the mood is Janed

You included me and it's
all over now
baby you.

So the job is
basically hiding
the real from her. I was made
for this.

Someday she'll
leaf through my
little leafettes.
My little things.
Tossed. Tussled.
Won after a night
or three thousand.

Erasure of girl
is a tricky little
business I've been
at for a few
centuries now.
It's all caught up
to us. Puffed
sleeves and push
ups everything is
elevated. Make it
higher and high
like bangs.

You thought
those eyelashes
would make you
look smarter
they make you
smart. Isn't that
how they draw

baby animals
the big head
just made for
TV.

I am not a
representative.
Someone else
represents me to
me. In the big
buildings they
make a speech
for us and in the
little buildings
we pick our
favorites like
flavors of sorbet
before heading to
the post office.
It's that small.

I'm here to write
a government poem.
Same as government
cheese. It's not the
best. Even gets a name.
I channel some Chicago
individual who used
to like lines like these.

Keep making and making
anymore. Been at it and
under it. Teaching prepositions

while propositioning in
position. You could get
troubled in the exchange.
Dust your dirt cut suit off
line the stripes night before
It's not enough to be warm
anymore you've got to
want it hot.

She's always wrong sometimes.
If I come back a small dog
give me to her as a gift
instead of dessert some night
driving into the farmsides
seeing families of animals
out one window and
nothing out the other.
Keep driving she said
with one hand on the wheel
one hand on the other
thing.

Grass and a tree with a tire swing were fine for active, growing kids. Once the youngsters reached college age, though, the family decided it was time for change.

Fanny Howe says: “I’m not a mother, I’m a man.”

It’s a man’s man’s man’s man’s man’s man’s world.

Jasper Johns says: “Take an object. Do something to it. Do something else to it. Do something else to it. Etc.”

The elephant & Gertrude Stein are together. The beer & the broccoli are one.

Within a few months, the garden became an oasis. A generous patio is also an outdoor dining room, where curving beds frame the space and offer soothing views from every angle.

+

Begging for attention, this back corner was a yawner. The driveway was perfect for seating but needed a party atmosphere makeover.

We’ve moved from laps to hands.

In the diorama of natural causes, the Cowboy is always wrong. Fly like an eagle, eat like a bird. The sun is a really good sign. American Airlines says: Be Yourself. Nonstop.

Check it out now. Cushy, deep seating with clean lines makes for a comfortable place for hanging out, while sheers suspended from supports create the ultimate chill zone.

+

This crumbling garage seemed to hold little promise for stylish live/work space.

We are coming of aging, like Ida Blooms.

These are the worst good times. We do not understand the disapproving tube, the man with a plan massaging like a beef a bee.

High Wasp & Fat White.

They say this course is called "Ocean Sensing." Of course.

The remodel enlarged the building to include a bathroom, loft, and a small roof deck, so it can double as guest quarters. It can also still function as a garage thanks to a set of glass-paneled Dutch doors opening on the plywood-paneled office side.

+

Before its transformation, tumbleweeds had more fun on this deck than people did. There was no privacy, no ambience, no plants—just minimal seating that offered a less-than-stunning view of the adjacent carport.

She says: I. Was. Out. To. See. My. Mother.

He says: I. Did. Not. Know. Why. I. Called. Her.

We say: Alls well—with them dogs.

This forgotten deck transformed into an enticing outdoor dining room.

+

Obsessing about the mullet
badge of shame. The only hair
that is half a hair. You didn't go
all the way with that did you,
couldn't quite cut the cut, or
grow the grow. The only
androgyny is halfsies. Half

boy she said on her way half
out the door with half a hair
flying low. From the side you
look like me. I tried. She cuts
her shorter and shorter hair nails
pants. He wears the party in the
rear. From the back I thought you
were much older. From the knee
I thought I could cut you down.
From the bangs I thought you

were on the fringes. I am looking
and looking for the female mullet
of my dreams. Shame. Why can't
you just be one thing and call me

back. Part your hair down the middle
and take out a comb and lick it in the
middle of the street and comb me

down where my cowlick won't calm.
Big daddy talks like that in the booth after an
all nighter. I remember the
kid there when she wasn't. Little red

stick of gum inside. Any art project that
calls itself eggs has got me right there.
I would have to voice this to make it plain.
How elitist of you to want a read instead
of a listen. Listen to me cries the baby text.
Read to me over and over. What mother says
you don't deserve it, here, pulls it out, whips the

shirt off her dragon scales climbing weighing over. Her
shoulder has penetrated itself in a bone buckle, two cakes
and two types of berries inside, this is the soft thing you put in
your mouth, here, not that, chomp. Another mother, not me, takes
her baby to the beach after the mother's mother begs and begs her to
take the baby to the beach and don't blanch it, don't botch this try. Take her
there, take her out, swing wide the blankets, free to kid in the sand, handfuls and

handfuls of sand and broken shells I am not worried about. I worry more like syringes
ok broken glass, fine, all the mothers I have not bonded with or boned inside and don't
agree, we will never agree, mothers and me. Why would you worry about that why
wouldn't you just get a different kind of kid. I want a new kind of kick. One who
doesn't shove it in. One without shovel hands from the outdoor. I didn't make
that kid, that is not my decision to make. You make dresses and put them
on the computer so I can find them and show them to mine in bed.

The computer is where you buy things. As long as I can stay in bed
the longest, this is where my portraits will be, my art school rainbow
plantings, the collage I pasted with my early general educational
kiddos in the back row, the ones who show midway through,

swing wide the saloon doors of my classroom are we in a
lockdown situation. I will document my documents and
messes, it takes me this long to make. We have been

colonized in our house by a half sized abnormal, not saying,
just emptying drawers and closets and every basket I house
you in spills over as if it was built to, as if a band named for a
bodily function, she has taken the house and upsized it with small pebbles
from shoes and rocks from socks, half a human half a life, half
of our drawers are empty the others have leaves and buds from unnamed
rosemary trees, jasmine she says as if knowing. Three sunflowers that are not,

only yellow and flower looking because petaled. Pink rocks from the big yard that
are more salmon and possibly human made. It is only half a thing to count the puppy
dog tails, the paper cut out doll parts, the stickless mermaid sticker hair and tails
and bandeau bikini tops, tulle is hanging over my eyes, bangs. I am half with it
and half out of milk. Not even answering the phone even if it is the school,
not even, how many ways will I be arrested today. Look at me from
the front and see me coming.

NOW

Architecture is an idea that you live in. Watching the puddle on the roof of the port like someone has watched it before. Like this cloud cover covers over clods and the one distant still building biding through distinctive medjool palms. It's all roofs. I've got all roofs from here and isn't that envy, *l'envie*, the idea of another's things. If I move my head a little to the right I can just make it. I can make out star-colored leaves leaving traces and leavening my sight line like a hem. I wear my eyes like a skirt. She had eyes the color of a newbie. A red empty vase sits hollow in the hand. You can make anything this way. Any. Thing. Why is it wrong to right into the spaces. Not space, not not a moon, not a new page, an old horizon. How many years did a woman live here before me. This is the question you ask yourself before moving in. Once you move in there is no moving anymore.

You can write about your kid but not your times. Mary Kelly. I can say she wakes up at night and says one funny word, one funny word every night, like salami or tic tac toe. I can say she puns but I can't remember them. They said her father was a word attacker. The same kindergarten teacher whose legs he massaged. I can say calamity but not daily. Who is allowed to say say anymore. This is not a body I am not part of. It's not that I wish I lived in Norway or no it's not that I'm going to live in Norway it's just that I wish I was born in Norway and I don't understand what all these Norwegians are doing here they are just fine thanks. Who needs what we have. What do we have, Nestlé. There are so few thoughts that go around and I am penned in my macadamia nut trees and that is what lasts and what I can talk about. Although apparently trees die after a time, like they don't just live forever which I had never considered.

I thought a tree dying was a sign of pestilence or terror or you'd done something wrong in your life and so your tree died. But no, sometimes, like a pet, they just go. Lifespan different than a dog, how unfair is that, you just get your dog for only this little finger of time and then move on. Whose pets are we? If the lifespan of a tree is significantly longer than ours, does that make us its pet? Like in the concentric circle of lifespans, who wins that contest and is that how you decided to make god a thing? Who am I asking all these questions of, my mother? I am the mother now and have to come up with answers like the way one letter from the word "now" to "not" changes everything: your breakfast is now ready, your breakfast is not ready. Why don't we speak typos. At the level of the letter. It's when I saw my hand holding the baby's head I realized I wasn't the baby anymore.

My hand looked human, feminine human, not mine, from a picture or a film strip. I come up with answers like because the wolfy dog wears a bandana or because nuts are hiding or because you are magic. Or because your grandmama didn't have any, or because planes are very far away, or because we all share one letter in our names. Me and you and me and him but not you and him which proves I am central. I need proof. Poof. I need to cut my nails down quick and shave my eyes or eyebrows as they call them and I would like a different color for hair but I can't decide, something that makes me happy but everyone else hates. I want something I can see but invisible to others. I am shocked on the radio when they still use light and dark / white and black to stand for good and bad, not even. Everybody does it. But me. Look at me. Being better. Than me.

What if reading Melville doesn't do it for me, what if I can't get beyond my critique of the male me I could be. When she asks why she asks it why why why why why, but pronounces whoy whoy whoy whoy whoy, so as to call attention to the very constructedness of the questioning word and its repetition, as if we are both in on the joke, the serious joke, of whyness. I can write about how she keeps one finger in her mouth or her nose in all photos but then I think of the person that is her and the words that will remain a trace and even if they go nowhere but here why would I want her to know her mother's own true thoughts, no one wants to hear that. It's like staring into the abyss of mise-en-abîme mirrors, or Sigourney Weaver in *Alien*, you will complode. If I do this every day does it make it daily. I barely brush my teeth, the floor is covered in jungle and Easter baskets and plastic grass from the neighbor. I made every point to get the recycled easy to clean kind and then in walks the better shinier plastic Easter grass that will never go away. What else do I see, what is around here. Without turning my back I know there are balloons on the ceiling and matching cards unmatched on the floor and typos in front of me where I can see. A family of plastic pigs shares space with unicorns, or alicorns, which is a stupid name for a pegasus unicorn. When should I tell her we almost named her Pegasus but I didn't like to call her Peg.

This is your last kitchen. How many people have that, think that, eat that thought for breakfast, take it out for a spin around the block. How many have a block. Are you trying to connect or resect. What is this body doing here and when do we get to stop asking that question. When your teeth aren't taken care of for you, nothing else matters. We spin around around in a pod like those cartoons drinking big gulps of a Big Gulp getting our nails colored inside the lines only. I was room parenting when you walked in. I had drawn big bubbly letters that said Sequoia Tree, making sure to correct the spelling, making sure not to lock the hatch on my way out.

Dress up. Ogle. Google. Capsize. I let the children draw all over the poster board, outside the lines of the letters S E Q U O I A T R E E. We related the facts to their sizes—one tree is 100 children tall, 1000 children old, 20 children around, the bark is 1 child wide. I made them sequoias poof. I was not parenting or rooming. What would Mary Kelly do and what would her child Kelly Kelly do. So she is mother plus child named. Half mother half child which seems fair. My father recently admitted that more genes come from the mother but they—mad males—have always wanted to say 50-50 just in case we rose from our ash beds and demanded our children back. How could we do such a thing we are too busy typing and on our phones, of which we own 5 billion, more than the people in existence when I was born.

We are too busy calculating our earned income credit or mortgage dividend or some other piece that will buy us a feathered boot which will open another door and create another obligatory bond. I hear noises outside the house, my building, and will run out the back door like the junkie nurse when I accidentally toured her apartment with her landlord. There she was shivering in the shower, then out the back, hiding under some steps, covering, what a view I am. The building makes the sequence. Closet, stairs, backness. I am not writing this I am thinking it. I did not think it before I wrote it. I did not make it I had an idea and then I did nothing and now I live under a tree. I am outside my body at least once a day. I see elephants running under the side of my eye, eaves until I realize it is traffic. I dream of rats under the floorboards and am pretty sure I am right about it, everything. Why do we mother: for once we have something, are needed, plus authority. We will never solve the puzzle this way and imaginary science will continue to ambush and colonize each wave, a puddle on the port just outside the view.

Mrs. Featherbottom calls me from below to ask if I can bring her some more. I tell her I have no more and am not in a bringing kind of way. I wish I told Mrs. Featherbottom that. I wish Mrs. Featherbottom called me anymore. There's not much below Mrs. Featherbottom if you're really calculating it out. We have two different kinds of decision making and no one is talking about the third thing. We used to shoot holes in our stories and now it's each other. Floors of cars in the rain. The small person here told me about what a balaclava is before I could even look it up. Don't tell me I said I want to look it up. Don't go ahead and know things already. Who said you could get here before me. Who is in the business of arriving. I will do this every day until I don't. I have found that is the perfect excuse for any occasion—it was working until it wasn't. I wanted this until I didn't. I was happy until. A small bear-covered dog sits on the floor expecting other animals to arrive. She is her own personal tea party. Someday good you'll get to be a fool again. Someday fool you'll taste a different kind of cobbler than Mrs. Featherbottom is offering. She's not offering anymore. I negate this I negate that. See how I built the thing while negating the thing. See how I can take away anything I want. How many ways do you want to understand that thing. I can take a way what I want. I didn't want it anyway.

The collected texts of my sister would read something like we miss you how are you are you hanging in there did you get my message have you called mom back did you answer aunt junebug's letter did you hear about aunt junebug did you know aunt junebug is homeless again did you know aunt junebug died. There is a definite skunkishness following me. Her. We could call it birdlike but that would be minimizing the pain. In the comparison of oppressions fastest wins. We have a rich history of saying no. That pulled me in right away. A song follows me in the room. I look up videos of other people singing it. I realize there is a film of me making good before film was a thing. There's a special kind of song that you care about so much you say Look I don't care what you do to me but this song, don't touch.

The screaming barnacle reeled her in. She was misspelling things today and there was only one way to say it. Say sea. Say she was overloaded with overboarders. She leaned way over, too far for folks who don't lean. Something grabbed her back and it was, as she said, that screaming barnacle. Not screaming in the audible sense. Just mouth wide. Open faced. Screaming in the sense of leaning into. Leaning so deep into as to go through. Leaning so far and deep into the throat of inaudible screaming as to become another mother on the other side. Isn't this what tubes are for, she thought, petting her digs. No her dogs. Her three poodles Noam Chomsky, Leon Trotsky, and Jhumpa Lahiri. On deck. I asked for a film with a deck chair and a boat and all I got was this pirate ship. She thoughts. Thinking aboard is thinking again. I am not thinking about you thinking about me. I am. Her three petted poodles and a deck chair over there. Over the edge of the cliff of the boat which is to say the silken mahogany railing. She gets deep into the description of mahogany to herself. It's a dark wood, a grandmotherly wood, the sign of a good home in a certain county of America in a certain century not this one. Can we pull these woods from that time into our own. Can we pull anything that is not burled. I have described the situation to myself for the rest of my life, she says, stalking down the silvered corridor stairs to the waiting audience whose backs are turned, looking ashore. We know enough about other times to make them again but not to make them make sense again. You know enough about me to recreate me on stage and screen but not page that's a tip too far. Please do not approach me when I am writing to the corporation. She pulls out, now, a nub topped pen and one of those hamburger erasers so thick with the early set. Toddlers, she knows, eat them up. This is now my audience, anyone facing left. I will determine whether or not you are audient. I will say. And I will ship the hell out of the shape to get it. She circles a round with her shoe's toe. A perfect oval no an egg in the deck. Almost a knothole. Some closed rotundity approaching the slender sphere. Are we talking a ship a the ocean or a ship a the stars. We've got oceans and oceans to burn. After we've exhausted everyone else. Push it out, into the middle, where you will a beached up poodle lay. If it wasn't for the galley barnacle that snagged her she'd be gone.

She wasn't about it. Wasn't about to walk the twelve counted steps into the dank basement to find some fly fishing treaties on the wall and give up then. She was a persister. That's what her sisters called her anyway. Stuck in a high lonesome suburb that was once a petunia grove that was once a bog for slave-owning sissies. She's not sure she can say that. Her parents have stocked their pantries with double sized bags of semi sweet chocolate chips that have nothing semi about them. This is supposed to be cozy. There is nothing but horror in a house with ten-year-old canned peaches and evaporated milks and no one home. Maybe these aren't her parents after all. Maybe she picked the lock on the wrong look alike box. The ticky tacky smells all right but won't get you high. She's here for the files.

Well I just picked up my rose and ran, that's all. In the south, when the down mouth stops you by the gutter, I get lost on the waterfront with cotton snakes. I forget to say I or Ah. That's very compassionate, I think. To treat the old man to my humor. Imagine him in the home with nothing left. Is that the only way to be kind. To some people. Some people. I ain't people. Some pictures of me aren't so hot. Like the ones in my bones shirt with no bra from the side and 3 months in. Let that be a lesson to the camera. Is this how it's going to go from here, telling it like a sauce. Waiting for her to come pick it up. I don't know, I'm new to space. Tell me something I can't hear.

She picked up the wrong mug, again, and carriaged on like nobody. What is that pelican doing on that red log, they all asked her. Why picking up flat toothpicks of course, the kind that are hard to find. There are no toothpicks in that red log, if it is even a red log. She solved the logical problem by leaving the chat room. Everyone applauded by typing Gggggg. She couldn't remember the first time she saw three planks of wood, but definitely the rainbow shoulder bag with the umbrella built in had something to do, and listening to Anne Murray and Crystal Gayle records on the industrial brown carpet with someone whose name she can't remember that started with Mrs. Several Jessicas, one with a hair lip possibly and overgenerous parents who clearly ruined her. A girl named Muffin whose parents ran. Someone else's who kissed in the kitchen. These were the insides then, nothing can change that. Even if she stops trying to remember anything at all, clear the pooch, stain clean the pavement, erase the bed she drew there, for lying down in. If her book could have drawings, they would be from above. Tight domestic spaces owned, with doorways and passages into each other's rooms, flat and bird's eye from up high. She would live there and be still.

In an old box you keep a few things. A butterfly from your father-in-law, a ticket stub from the Zombies show, some Bazooka Joe. This places you. You have no such box, you have no such memories. You had a record player once that was a suitcase. Just like I used to be a girl. Not like that at all. You heard the story at your father's retirement party, the last time you tried to dress civvie and pass for daughter. You got that periwinkle polyblend button down blouse and high waist black wool skirt with the impossible slit at Bebe at the mall with money from your mother. You can't believe what size you are. You get a chunky stacked 1930s heel. You haven't worn heels in years, since you escaped the south. You're 20. You're about to move west, to Seattle, like everybody except you don't know that. You try not to hate everything but you do. Then someone tells you about his greatest accomplishment. At this penis fest celebrating the penis doctors and their standby penis-less wives.

There's a story five ways to not tell it. You were raised by Gertrude Stein in a subway surrounded by knitters. You grew up among the thieving class and push-up specialists. They come at you now with knives over air mail. It's a symbolic cousin that gets the prize. A story of no stories. Can you tell a thing without the thing. Or the tell. It's just words, they'll say. So's that. What else is there. What else is here. The more confident your steps in sync with the sound of your throat, the more impervious to critique or friendship. Requests from the long side of the cabin. A dog licks herself next to you on one spot. Many spots. An animal is always being licked. If you could figure out the puzzle you wouldn't be so smart. It's not a puzzle at all, not even a game or a gamer. It's a straight shot down the gullet. You remembered something else for the list.

I take pictures of dangerous things. I take a snap of a blady knife perched peeking the edge of the countertop but what kind of countertop I am rememembering wood marble fake stone linoleum formica. Once I saw a saw sitting out in the sun. Lying in decomposed granite I protected dogs like human babies as if they would run and fetch and not note the handsewn edges waiting to bite the pup feet that feeds them. Weighing the truth and accuracy of my dangers is a full-time gig. I am measuring my ometer. I didn't know they had helmets for that part. I figured cotton was safer as a bet. Until pesticides came into the picture. I get an image of insides turned out and hey I'm just trying to keep us sewn up here. If you start spilling they might not believe you anymore or let you near the buffet. As they say. I wasn't built for this, I had an extra shell when I came out, candy coated, thick as rice. They say you want back in well I just want a flak jacket, a wooden suit, a hiding dress with pockets, lace up boot sleeves, red pleather earmuffs, rock candy eye goggles, a zipper up the back for easy release, and a twenty-two-inch pile of steel, melty in the middle, for forming.

Show me a depressed mother and I'll show you a mother. No, I cannot break that down. Cannot excise or as they say snip snip. Mothers walk around with their bags open saying As they say. The rat light goes out behind me. I am a me in here, holding the bag and carrying on as if. The trolley comes my way and I see a man in pain. I am not concerned about him, he wears shorts and rubs his legs, ok maybe I am a little concerned. I am seeing these things through a window as if for the first time, but telling you here, who knows. I never answered that phone call. I never picked up the green cord and twisted it around my little finger and drew candy corns and candy canes all over the doodle pad even onto the counter top all over the telephone and scrawled under the table to the carpet oozing all over things even I am not supposed to touch, and I am the mother, so I get a say. I was that way before this was even a problem and you barely noticed, I swam on by in my pool of pills, no I mean really, the pool I swam in, right below the kitchen window, the spaces we spend our time. If you don't think girls belong in the front of the club, then you never. You never walked and talked.

There was once a lot more of you. In your tights walk the walking plank across the floor, make a move, turn your feet into a pie. Today you made history, America, we are so used to saying, can I put it on a t-shirt, can I slogan out of your line like a peel, pluck me sticker, the magnet won't stick I have nothing metal made of me. Once you were made of wood, this is a library riddle, and you came back an app and bit us and clung and drew juice. I hadn't tried to say anything into the headset before now, hadn't called you president before, and here we are in bed again, writing reading eating watching not watching. I am not holding anything in my hand, here you are unfolding. Once things were made of cotton and we were allowed to see so, clear down through the glass bottomed boat before we bottomed out. I am trying to tell you what happened but your cruise control won't call me back. We were at the top and that was the problem, the were, the top, the we.

I can only imagine what they're talking about in the impeach jar I opened, canned, burnt past recognition, a pale muse of what once was, say to the dying boy, be a man. Is that your answer to the global crisis or are we talking more of a striding by the grocery with a kid unhooked in a stroller. How dare you accuse me of domestication, this is the stuff of humanity, just because you're not in my 51% don't make it out of me. If you believe I was made from a pomegranate biter then I've got another book to sell you, and this one replaces all the pronouns with opposites and middle opposites and what does that do to your belief then. Does your belief depend on me to open it, crack that nut like a slow-moving rat on the line, does it.

Today is the fifth day of the rest of my wife. If I were to sit across from you in the board room, meeting room, interview and say read me, fine, tell me all the things, you could say, card shark, first, then blond card shark, then trickster, muffin, potato acer, ship runner, overland comer, movie longer, Garbo hoarder, with a wrinkle under your so's your uncle for your favorite rock. I am looking forward to a time when I can compete. Until then, I am slavering in the mix and no I don't know what that means but it won't stop me from translasting it. I was born for it, you say, this movie is great, it's got a crazy lady, you say, you're not a turnip. I like that very much.

You've got the brains I've got the books let's lose lots of money. It's all come down to shade. Shadow fill in the blanks and box checker, is that the new dead job, the one they're handing out with diplomat diplomas these d-days. Did you just say disciple or am I fantasizing again. Like at the grocery in line for crepes and the little boy with the twister shirt on begins to sing into the microphone like he never left it. There I go again you say, what is it with the world and percentages. I am nine times nine of myself and still too much. If he wasn't that kind of doctor what would he be. This referent refers to nothing and I draw a tree to prove it. You and I decided these rules long ago when we were babies, the babies of humanity, decided it all. That might not be the problem.

What are you folk she asks herself asking herself down the hall. It's not a way, not a way of asking that we're asking for, it's not a folk I'm addressing, am I even dressing, sometimes you can even know what she is talking about, isn't that amazing. I can't hear you, we say to me, I can't understand what you're looking for and what you're after and isn't your language just private language and we can't understand you anyway can you speak up. I am speaking up says the little old lady inside me. Can't you just stand there and be pretty and get younger a little bit instead of challenging my perception of linguistic associative behaviors and cultural competencies which I thought I had maneuvered myself around inside the pantyhose stricture of the system that has been decided before you got here, I was dancing down the hallway inside the leotard of my brain when of a sudden a snag on the nylon stopped me in track 2 and I switched it up to another, slower, roundabout, a sly lick of the knife, a shady touch off the side thumb, peel it off, it's only skin, I said, what are you, what are you doing here, I said listen, ask me before asking me if.

I am formal parenting. This guy talks like a rebus. She wears her face like Sesame Street. You want to have a conversation. About the way that I am. I saw my faces in the photograph and I knew. It's because of this apron isn't it. The one I was born with. Phases are clearly meaningless. The man on the news asks me why I said why I said. Can she take him down and still stand. Can I talk about the tree, the tree you used. If I point to your bumper sticker to prove my point does that make me like you. I am corralling human. I haven't decided if I am the cookie box or the cookie. I am a moving crisis in Washington and the kids know it. Watch me watch you corrupt the process. Main justice is like the little dick in the big room. Sticking the landing and strolling.

Everything has a lot to do with my brother. My brother's mother. When I say formal parenting I mean filling in the form. When can you use form and have it be good. When my body is there and my eyes are not there. I am here for you, form you. I listened and I was sitting down. My hands were pasted to each other in listening posture of listening. I was not listening I was sitting down. My hands were massaging each other lightly you could not see. I was cleaning the toilet in my mind, of my mind. You were the child but not for long.

Tendu does not mean "to stretch." The four-year-old leg and its grammar. Only fours in here petits. It's a jolly feet no wiggles. These are exercises we lose our breaths. Yes no broken crayons. Hand on bar on hip on point. Look at my feet look at me. What do hands do pique to prick. Face me turn around you don't even have to think about it. Only we can draw pretty pictures. What is the front of you. Relax. I could really sing something if there were more activities.

In the morning, valentines. When we rise from our corn cribs. I saw a bed in the corner of the writer's room that she was sharing with the magazine and I wasn't sure whose bed it was, hers or the story's. Writers write about their spaces saying they colonize them. This table has been taken over from that child and no meals will be served until this chapter is finished. Valentines will not be made. I have a crafty kid which means she wants to make things out of pieces whole. All the plastic one used in one's life has come back to live in the living room.

Written on the wind with Robert Stack and Lauren Bacall are not being shaken or stirred they are loading the plane with this kind of Lucy and everyone together in the cockpit makes for a cozy pilot indeed. I've seen you before, at the office he says, and how long have you known Mitch. This is the part where the anti-daddy's boy becomes someone else's daddy's boy and Daniel Boone is thrown around loosely. Is your daddy a big man, bigger than a big book. Here is where she falls for him because he stinks. How much devil can one girl hold in her and who is put to shame. I love the person I talk to. Three thousand or thirty above the regular peaches we got to know each other and then we didn't. Tell me something Rock Hudson, the name is synonymous with hooky. We checked into the hotel, all together now, a suite with pink walls and clothes in every size, just in case we grow.

We could keep going like this I suppose, a gold beaded bag is everything. Open the closet door yourself, I'll furnish the hats. I am three behind where I should be and real breathing is really happening in my room. I like your breathing I say to my kid in grateful yellow. We floored each other. It's not a crack. This is serious and she is different. Who would have spit in whose eye and are you decent. Who is the arbiter of my purple rooms. White roses and cheese, statues, trays, magnums on chill. I got on the flight, coach, like sliding into a bath. Take me off of here, never take cream, up in the blue, I won't like any of these things in the morning.

She walked down the hall in a revised step, I would say gait, but she was staring at cows and that seems a little too nosy. Like tom dick and harry asking for dates, each other, a wife and a home and kids, I mean the delicacy, have you got a date, I'd like one. And so she was married near a yellow chair and no one cared to say a few words about the wedding. Just a girl, a lady, and I've got news for you. What kind of Miami do you go for and is this the part where the groom sleeps in and we see her face a blank. She didn't like the way she walked and so she switched it. I won't sleep with things in the bed anymore.

It’s tempting to abstract it. It was under our feet all the time. Tight under the soil where the rats lay their nuts. When is a rat a dog. I wasn’t getting the mail anymore, wasn’t even checking. Sometimes you walk down the hill and it’s covered in nuts and oranges, blossoms and shells. Like a perfect diet. When we gather here together we gather in nut. The neighbors were popping over the fence, just a pop in to say hello and check on our carpets. There are ways to ask questions and then there are ways to dominate someone with question marks, to push them into little hills of ant sand with every q, for which there is no a.

You could say it and say it. You have all your little things. Here we are in our little things. I have a sliding door. I have two. My sidle is surrounded. Animals, nuts, people. Lonely is other people. Everyone is supposed to think about someone. How often do you account for else. An else. Let's call her Elsa. If she is. If she even is.

You have to say how the other side won. You have to say Martians and Confederates. If you are really to be a scientist of the word you have to say it. Say I will not get too specific so as to let you in but specific enough so as to invite you in. Say it doesn't matter what you say. Someone won't believe you. Put on a jacket and try again.

Maybe if you covered up the collar. A little more on top. Try so as not to look like trying. Follow from the rare essential middle. Get yourself an exposed midriff and grow up a little. Every 5 year old needs to get with it. Get over it and yourself at the same time on the seesaw. I saw some bad ones in the sand once. Good baddies. The lots are full of them.

They take it a little far. I haven't even considered you yet. I applied. You think I'm talking about it when I'm talking all around it. There in your little snow hut in the sun. There there in it. There was an audio file once of the audiophile in the wind. You couldn't understand him for the blowing.

If you're going to go synoptic make sure it's short. Like a hem. Some cats are bigger than others. I have to make space on the bench for you and me and everyone we see. There is always more space if you could up. Layers. Pile on. Stuff stuff in. Riding high in the clown car of humanity. I have envisioned all the places so hard it burned my blue light through.

Metal roof. Vintage wallpapers. Days before the kitchen motto. A patch of grass leading to a meadow to a hillside frolicked through with straw flower. No one could describe the island better on top of it or inside. Two famous people come from there with red hair. If a cat don't know he don't know.

I can't fake the word count. I take the examination for admission to the government body. I take it well. I take it for the one behind me. I take it for the next in line and next to her too. I decide only one person can take the tests for all people and we will all pore our scores over the water fountain. Women like myself. Trouble.

Some people don't like authority. At the level of the letter. Changed it from inside the box. Came out a tin can. This thing I am teaching you is a waste of your talents I say. The thing is in the future. In the future there will be none of this. None of this reading and writing saying did she just say that. You're not so special. Just in time.

Her gloves are off. Covered in pox. By the door in a small handmade satchel with a velvet string. The door slides off. She skips lunch. Picks her teeth with twigs and nails. Forms a basket of her hands. Covers up. Goes upside down. Thrashes lightly in thin air. Feels better.

Turning the thing over and over like a desert covered coin. There are certain places where things are better. Our passports don't work there. It's not that we're trapped it's that we're fallen. The announcement came over the paper cup phone. Stay in your pod small ones the invisible airborne monster we told you would never come came. Don't worry, it's not in the closet. It's in your mouth.

Am I specific enough for you. Did you hear me taking care of everything. Did you notice I already set it out. Fixed it up. Placed each item side by side in the box with a clean cloth between. Remember to loop the straps over your wrists so you can carry more. Don't forget the things I told you that you didn't hear didn't listen didn't want to know yet. Remember all the parts in the middle. Forget the end.

At first things were fine. Great even. Some might say wonderful in an email. Might look up alternatives like magnifique. When she learns how to say splendid the game is begun. The pink parts got lost under some furniture. Piles of dusty. Once a friend called and you stared and stared at it like an open letter. No, a bill. You don't answer those any more. Not until the collection comes.

We are in the thick of the steak meat now. And I mean our own. Raw on the sides but fairly well familiar to the tooth. Stringy sinew and stingy bone. The velvet cup meat is best enjoyed cold. How do they talk about flesh and if they had to stop eating it or die we know the answers. They would build entire systems designed to falsify records and distract with more visible natural disasters like elementary school or fairgrounds with nothing but corn cake around the animal. Sweet surprise.

A shooting is a matter of opinion apparently. I'm just saying what you thought. I had a failure of elimination. It could only be predicted. All the statistics were on our side. We were so right, so dying.

I can see the other side from here. It's just a walk across a faulty bridge. Keep doing what you do well which is bare minimum. You are good at nothing. And I mean that in the most meaningless way possible. Watch the hole in the covered part over the ravine. That's where they decide future tax credits to pay for all the pillage.

There is nothing to check anymore. I've read all the updates and the scroll just stopped. All caught up here. Nothing new. Got that out there in time. Piled up the thumbs. Quick a button.

Could do this all day. Did.

NOW

I'll try this hour
to turn this thing
another way
they say retire
late and keep
the cash this time
It's a short step
to claustrophobe
I had fear of moon
I read it said it's
uncommon good
to run around a
round miss Mary
Astor's asters

They say Credence is
the best American band and
I am in its pocket now
First of now a first of may I
Decembered poem in the pile
Movember may be better
than June for roasting huck
nuts but soon it's a line like
that that will get you kicked
out of Johnny B's in a hot
March may I make a
suggestion a pill is not
my name too bad she said
keep driving the car with
no hands and I will surfeit
something out of it serve
it up good I sung from the
back loud and clingy
hear my hymn

Sometimes I can't look
at people on tv, the snug
faces black glasses back
at me, a needle pointing
poing into this room, a cody
hung on a chair, sunny faucets
facts on a forehead, I can't bear
it up, the watching. Listen
if you don't like what you got
you can sin again, against the
wing I keep buried. Cover my
peepers with your fat buckle
so I can't see the newest war
the bear unleashed, the trash
covered weather map I wear.

Clear the shelves he say
saying the mononuclear
runon. I can use this and
use that undergarment
bag I think thinking thin.
Planes take on and off
again after the rush
pushing one foot into
the other time zone.
I let the kid make sprinkles
in the slush, angels by
the needle exchange
by the yard. At least
a nickel a pill will
yielding come in swinging
singing all clear, the tan
man sneaks you in the view.

I have no exhaustion left
a trill a minute seeker
miles to go to go apres
du sun. Who sais so I
sai she can her mother
and I do. Immuno stuff
and the left, how unfair
are we how similant.
Someone claimed right
left you to your own
raging ringing I want
to say with that shitty
slutty merman under
the sea.

Only the credits can
make Johnny live again
You lunked up the hill
to the extremist musem
We'll no more ravish
the tea than we will the
Clydesdale, these things
thinly swelled. A topper
a passioning hair, this
museum makes odds
on the future rivers rose.

I have 35 items in my cart
What is an item
You ask
What is a cart
Boys aren't allowed
to look so beautiful
I am liquid and avail
able she says when she
listens to your son
playing with her
toys without her
home. I will buy
you anything you
want just don't
leave me alone
leave me alone.

Live by the snow drop
Wait by the fire
We are cradle to graving
it every time we sing
Take my pocket and the
kid within it, strike a match
to show your rage. This
bumper sticker or that
face stamp, we've got
you covered in ink spilled
all over the highway
in the middle of an island
by the stump in the trench
you wear out the inside you
wore out, you repeated
yourself twice and shook
hands with the wrong guy
on the right side. We foil
ourselves like cartoon
bandits. America are you
listening, lingering, are you
so old you can't just can't anymore.

Honeysuckle was her name
A green house on a land
mine in an empty town
Who cares about that
anymore. Twelve times
twelve is just something
you learned once, like
the way I said that
in a voice all your own.
This must be your month
Over the pipeline around
the crick past the possum
to the empty yard
it's full of people.

Slow the prod
Slow the slowmo
Further mem a hot take
You've got the hot hand but
once a year so take it
Sit by the river and chew
Those catfish come up
for grub every time we shake
it, stocked and bottom fed
a handful of pre-evolutionary
scum, like something you call
someone at a bar. Take it back
the photo you took at a wedding
once, a long driveway where someone
else grew up. Boys call it pond fudder,
better than none, chugga choo
hit the brakes, pick a memory
it lives longer.

It only works if you're mad
I can't make up some cloud
to carry the loud sounds
I took a minute in there
I watered it down
I held my breath my nose
the handle I shook to see
what was left.

Every body has one because
here we are, the steam of that
email train was perpetual
and in motion, we will not
end it. Because that's a good
one. Every body turns one
on at a time, trust me, when
my pants are on I cannot tell
a lie.

She painted the faces
of all her animals
and called them
sticky stuck in a tree,
belonging there, made
to be a shirt a monster.
This one was born to be
one. The others looked
at me like too loud
get back, over here,
a goat, small dirt,
tiny bear, leafless.
These are the words
a mother spells
with a licking stick.
Someday you'll be old
you'll like it.

I say I have only
this BMW yoga mat
to call my own.
I seem like one
of those people
who die young.
I seem to myself
like one.
Boomers
who mourn their
dead at 87, 89, 91
don't say "from me
to me" anymore
and we don't say
"you don't say"
these days but
you sure got
a lot
out of a little
on this rock.

I got untired
watching the gif
I watch the bubble
dance inside his green
balloon, I watch
his purple friend
on the floor make
a worm of himself
and others. I have
been afraid so
afraid before.
I am sore
for the men
inside their empty
puffy suits. I have
never coughed like
that or moved my neck
so little. I worry
the dancers won't
check themselves
at the door.

Everywhere is
a new kind of baby
popping up in pop
up shops and flip
books, new hands
sewn with lots of
little details, beadwork
and leather. They hated
what they were wearing,
the new babies, they wanted
something less. They feel
if they could stop this
menace they could do
anything. We don't have
the heart to read them
the news.

Women of the 1940s
write 20 books before
they die of throat cancer
at 69. Mostly mysteries
suspense thrilled cat box
bunglers harpsichord
mixups slaptick pill bos
three penny heartaches
fortuneteller romances
circus joy thumbwarmers
ten times the charmers
knock the door down
I killed a thousand cows
in my roll me up obsessive
Ford fandango. Sometimes
they publish poems and win
national prizes like the Yale
but no one remembers them
even me.

American girls no
girls in the library
we filmed it so it’s
happening or made.
I feel under the dam
sounds romantic
never say “or” or
go on tv don’t be
live on your own
stay in the closet
and breathe

Second try to reach
the cord I plucked
a live one from out
of the station and
made this out of
that. We tried once
more to convince
our ponies of trying
times together. Once
more a second cough
cough means don't
say it don't say
nothing.

Hand over to this
body a handful
of sand be a baby
inside the grass.
It requires sips
and sips of wet
images pulled
as in stretched
to a feather to
be neutral in time
we have not
agreed to agree to
an inclining individual
this is not the trial
I was looking for
when I signed up
for soccer not ice
skating you looked
at me twice and lied
lied it down in the short
sand be a mixy one take
your bottles out and stand.

I'm pretty sure this
is going really well
the wall is slick and
the cows are ready
I took a hammer to
that idea and moved
in closer. Inside the
photo booth. One
party is ready to go
to the mistresses
An eyeball inside a
bottle ship, a twig
stuck to a shoegum,
subprime steaks left
on the counter, six
rubber duckies

Boy sneakers and sea
rocks don't add up
besides it's locked
I go there all the time.
Why does the one white
wave flash soapy over
kid feet whenever you
stand lying. We didn't
find anything but loud
wind in the windows.
I thought the water
looked like milk on
the pebbles, a washed
up kind of looking
sister, but I was wrong.

Izou was the word that came
wrapping up my way when I
typed you the word input or
was it influx or impactful. We
are not allowed to use these
empty containers for full think
it shows we are unstable, culp
able, and wide legged in our
logics and anti stances like
stacy in the meadow ripping
it up and griping about how
many times she has been per
mitted, often, to return, to re
strain herself from the heather.
Please stop emailing me if you
want to be friends anymore.

Not not
Not now
Now not
Now now
Noot noow
New non
Noy noyt
Newt nein
Now no
Noo ny
Nee nun
Nee knee
Now now
No no
Not now
Now

Not yet she says
screams from the
inside of a porcelain
mug in the shape of
a unicorn the size of
a fist. Nono she screams
says stuck on the pink
seat the color of her
inside. Why are they
wearing pussy hats
in the color pink this
year that's not the
everyone color at
all. I can't stand
the screaming can't sit
through the noise
we're not going to
have this conversation
anymore this conversion
therapy is hurting my
likes. She didn't say it
I did. I remember a time
when my shoulders
weren't here but here.

The glitchy kitten
seeks the pea.
Seek it, seek it,
glitchy kittie.
Because what
is a day. Driving
in the car and in
the bed proscenium
forever on our own
sides, we watch the
movie our faces side
side side. I am I in
context. Never be
afraid of yourself the
sign says, never be.

Cookie I said
I say it for me
cookie was it
then oo and oo
oo I didn't know
you had another
way to say cookie
until I did. That
wasn't right I
rhymed rhyming
again like I did
in the old century.
Took it off and
then away a
sandy-colored
girl in pieces a
lively lonely Marilyn
in dresses a waste
of time and empty
spaces. Say it.

Sometimes you meet
a mom and think I need
to get my kid in a different
school. It's not that she's
responsible for gender
genocide she just is.
The path to passing
this pathetic class just
got morbidly more
reciprocal. Turn up
my nose at myself
in my Volvo nowhere
near Sweden. I can
not hate you more
when you are near
me valentine.

The sun king is my
copilot. A made man
on a pay phone at the
smoke shop in black
and white. Philosophical
restaurant menus are in
in the new year. Who is
that gentleman with the
monocle I met. In the
booth three desiring
fabled tea totes. We
do what we can do
when we can do what
we do without doing
what we can. Madam
please play with me
a minute more, just
another summer goes.

The chump punches
the clock each time
to show how bad it
is. Got ordered.
Kissed by a striper
I mean slip it. Every
day a man turns to
crime to avoid the
9 to 5 in some dumb
movie. The girls tie
the boss down and
yee haw their way
around the coffee.
How much would it
take to get you to say
we equal each other,
in and out of line.

Giant mother a
father for a day
relax your mouth
papa don't say a
thing until you say
rabbit rabbit. Show
me the picture of
a man in a car and
I will show you the
picture of a maybe
father maybe alone.
These trees allowed
us to call them baby.

ACKNOWLEDGEMENTS

"Bewilderment as a poetics and an ethics."—Fanny Howe

First and most gratitude to Ben, the original reader, the ever best. And to Wild Alphabet for reminding me to thank her.

Much heart-filled thanks to the brilliant Rescue Press poet-writer-editor-designer magicians, including Daniel Khalastchi, Sevy Perez, and Alyssa Perry, with extra special gratitude to the inimitable genius Caryl Pagel, my very own baggage-free Pound.

Part of this book was published as a chapbook titled "I'll Try This Hour" from above/ground press, edited by the generous and tireless rob mclennan.

Always gratitude to the hard-toiling editors (also writers) of the following publications, where pieces of this book first appeared:

[What if reading Melville], [This is your last kitchen], [Dress up. Ogle. Google. Capsize.], [We are too busy calculating], [Mrs. Featherbottom calls me], and [The collected texts of my sister] were published in *Action, Spectacle*.

[She walked down the hall], [It's tempting to abstract it], [You could say it and say it.], [Maybe if you covered up the collar], [If you're going to go synoptic], [I can't fake the word count], and [Her gloves are off] were published in Black Sun's *Digital Vestiges*.

[Grass and a tree with a tire swing were fine] was published as "Fairy Tale of the Suburban Makeover" in *Fairy Tale Review*, *The Yellow Issue*.

[Sometimes I can't look], [I have 35 items in my cart], and [Live by the snow drop] were published in *Fence* magazine.

[Today is the fifth day of the rest of my wife], [You've got the brains I've got the books], and [Flaming in the installation] were published in *Harp & Altar*.

[You can write about your kid but not your times.], [My hand looked human], and [The screaming barnacle] were published in *LAdige*.

[Architecture is an idea that you live in] was published in *Mantis*.

[Am I specific enough for you], [At first things were fine], [We are in the thick of the steak meat], [A shooting is a matter of opinion], [I can see the other side from here], [There is nothing to check anymore], [Could do this all day. Did.] were published in *Pamenar Magazine* with accompanying audio.

[I wish that I knew what I know] and [The difference between the news / reporters] were published in *periodicities*.

[I thought a tree dying] is featured on the Poetry Foundation's podcast *Poetry Now* and on poetryfoundation.org.

[Show me a depressed mother], [There was once a lot more of you], and [I can only imagine what they're talking about in the impeach jar] were published in *Touch the Donkey*.

The 16 pieces beginning with [I had to stop stop] through [It's good good good] were published as an ekphrastic poem based on Daniel Gustav Cramer's 16-photograph series "Stuart Highway, Northern Territory" in *Triple Canopy*.

NOTES

Pieces beginning with "Grass and a tree" and ending with "This forgotten deck" include the following found language from *Sunset* magazine:

"Grass and a tree," "Within a few months," "Begging for attention," "Check it out now," "This crumbling garage," "The remodel enlarged," "Before its transformation," "This forgotten deck."

Sandra Doller is the author of several books of poetry, prose, translation, and the in-between from the most valiant small presses. Her work has recently appeared in magazines such as *Fence*, *Harp & Altar*, *Pamenar*, and *Action, Spectacle*. Doller is the founder of an international literary arts journal and independent press, *1913 a journal of forms*/1913 Press, where she remains l'éditrice-in-chief. She lives in the USA, for now.